Blackout!

Written by Frank Pedersen
Illustrated by Graeme Tavendale

Contents   Page

Rigby

Blackout!

With this character ...

Hayley
Carlotta

"Suddenly, a

Setting the scene ...

This fiction story is based on some terrifying facts! The sun is a star and, like all stars, is made up of incredibly hot, swirling gases. Sometimes, these gases are whipped up into huge solar storms. These storms release enormous bursts of energy from the sun's surface.

Because there are only eight minutes before an energy burst hits the surface of the earth, there's no warning!
The staff of a power plant is about to be surprised by the effects of a solar storm. Engineer Hayley Carlotta is about to be caught right in the middle of it, and her ordinary day will be turned into one of the worst days of her life.

:03 p.m., it happened."

Chapter 1.

I've always been interested in stars
—the space type, not the people type.
Even when I was at school, I used to
look at the stars and wonder what they
were named, what they were made of,
and what it would be like to visit them.

Later, in college, I learned
more about stars and how they worked.
But I never imagined that the nearest
star to Earth, the sun, would have
such a major impact on my own work
—until tonight.

It's almost midnight. It's been the longest night of my life! My name is Hayley Carlotta, and I'm an engineer. Some engineers design bridges or buildings and some work on cars or planes. I work in a power plant that produces electricity.

Before tonight's adventure, it was hard for me to imagine what would happen if there was no electricity in our town. Everyone needs electricity for so many purposes—for heating and lighting our homes and schools, for cooking food, for working on computers, to communicate with each other, and many other uses.

Sometimes you don't even realize how much people depend on electricity—until, all of a sudden, it stops. When the electricity goes out, so does every single item that runs on electricity!

Chapter 2

Twelve hours ago, at noon, everything was working fine at the power plant. We were supplying electricity to all our customers.

What no one knew was that a major natural disaster was about to happen. And when it did, we would all realize how much we depend on each other, and on electricity.

Since school, I had known that the sun was a huge ball of gas. I knew that the sun produced enormous amounts of energy. What I didn't know was that the sun is not just quietly sitting there, burning away.

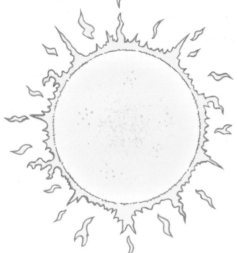

It has huge storms and gigantic whirlpools that send enormous bursts of energy into outer space. And every eleven years, it has a really bad storm! We were about to find out that this was the eleventh year!

Even if we could have known what was about to happen, we would have had only eight minutes' warning. That's how long it takes for energy to travel 93 million miles from the sun to the earth. But we had *no* warning.

Suddenly, at 3:03 P.M., it happened.

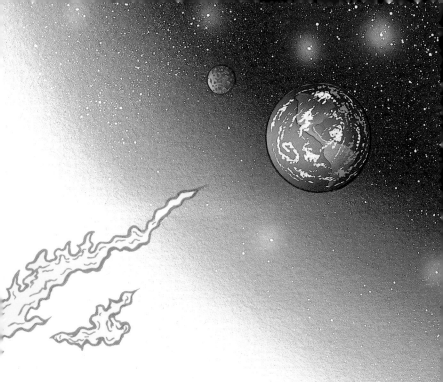

An enormous storm on the sun caused a huge burst of energy. That energy exploded away from the sun, and moved toward Earth, traveling at 186,000 miles a second. That's as fast as anything can travel in the universe. There was no getting away from that!

Eight minutes later, at 3:11 P.M., I was working in the control room of our power plant. It was a big cement-block room with no windows. There were maps of power lines with lights flashing and computers humming as they printed out data. There were controls, dials, and television monitors.

Suddenly, without warning, there was nothing. *Everything* went dead. No lights. No computers. No power. We were sitting in total darkness.

Chapter 3.

Later, I found out that the burst of energy had damaged all the power lines and electric equipment in our area.

All around town, the lights went out. So did everything else. Because we couldn't produce any electricity at the power plant, nothing that was plugged into a socket would work.

I reached for the phone. Luc[...] most phones did not need to be plugged in to work.

I called everybody I could think of to find out what was going on. It was disastrous everywhere. People were panicking! How could we get the electricity going again?

In the stores and offices around town, nothing was working. In the super-markets all the refrigerators went off. None of the cash registers worked. None of the fire alarms or security alarms were working.

In people's homes, TVs, stoves, and central heating stopped working. All electric clocks stopped at 3:11 P.M. I bet all the kids in school wished that it had happened *during* schooltime!

By 3:30 P.M., all the phone lines were busy. Everybody made phone calls to find out what was happening. Many of them called our headquarters at the utility company to complain! Many felt scared or worried.

I hoped that there weren't any emergencies for the police, fire department, or hospitals. With all the phones busy, emergency calls wouldn't get through.

Chapter 4.

I knew that some of the important services around town, like the hospital, had their own generators to supply electricity in an emergency. So did we—but it was only big enough to run a few lights and our main computer.

By 3:45 P.M., everything was back to normal at the hospital. Our computer was running again, too. The airport also had an emergency generator— nobody wanted airplanes to crash into each other during a blackout.

The other engineers who worked at our power plant rushed to work when we phoned them about the disaster. Most of them were here by 4:30 P.M.—except for one upset engineer. He called on his cell phone to say he had run out of gas, and the pumps at the gas station weren't working!

During the next hour, other power plants around the country called each other. The same problems were happening in cities across the area. We now knew that it wasn't something in our own power plant that had broken or burned out. This problem was much more serious than just a broken piece of machinery or a burned-out power cable.

But we didn't have time to figure out what had caused the problem. We just needed to get our power plant running again—quickly.

We all worked as fast as we could to check all the equipment in the power plant. We needed to start producing electricity really fast. Otherwise, we would have a lot of angry people in town! At that time, nobody knew that it was the sun that had created all our problems. Within the next two hours, the sun disappeared over the horizon, and everything began to get dark. *Really* dark!

We worked and worked and worked. At 8:30 P.M., we heard police sirens in the distance and wondered if there was trouble in town.

No street lights, no lights in the stores, and no security alarm systems meant one thing: The police were on the lookout for burglars!

Chapter 5.

By 9:30 P.M., all the equipment, all the power lines, and all the machinery had been checked and double-checked. Everything looked fine. We had repaired our cables. We had tested all the electric circuits. We were very tired. We were also hungry and thirsty.

I went to the vending machine and had to laugh at myself.

Of course, I couldn't get any cans of juice out, no matter how much money I put in. The vending machine needed electricity, too, and it wasn't plugged into the emergency generator. I couldn't make coffee or use the microwave to heat anything up. I wished I had made a sandwich before I came to work!

At 9:45 P.M., we decided to try to start up the generators again. All the engineers gathered in the control room, holding their breath as the switches were turned on. The generators began to hum. We hoped they would work. They had to work!

Slowly, our generators began to work, and we gradually increased the power. By 10:00 P.M., we were producing electricity again. Street by street, you could see lights glowing again all over town. I bet all those hungry, thirsty, and cold people out there were cheering!

I checked our main computer and saw that other power plants in the area were generating electricity again, too.

As life slowly returned to normal, we all relaxed. We had done our job and the electricity that every person in town relied upon was available again.

Chapter 6

It was only when I was listening to the car radio on the way home that I found out the facts.

Scientists from around the world were very excited about what had happened. Astronomers were being interviewed, and experts were being asked to help plan for any more emergencies like the one today.

I was just so tired. I hoped that my electric blanket wouldn't take too long to warm up!

I made a promise to myself that I would always keep some food and drink in the drawer of my desk, just in case there were any more emergencies.

I crossed my fingers and hoped that, in eleven years' time, when the next huge storms start up on the Sun, we will be better prepared.

Some energy bursts from the Sun have caused major power outages for days at a time.

In the winter of 1998, some parts of Canada were left without power for many weeks in freezing weather, because of power plant failures.

Energy bursts have also caused major short-term problems in the United States and in other parts of the world.

Although it was not caused by the Sun, New Zealand's biggest city, Auckland, had no power for weeks in 1998 because cables supplying all the electricity to the city broke. Millions of dollars of damage was caused.

Storms on the Sun happen every eleven years. Space engineers are planning to build and launch a satellite that will sit between the earth and the Sun to warn us of energy bursts traveling from the Sun to the earth.

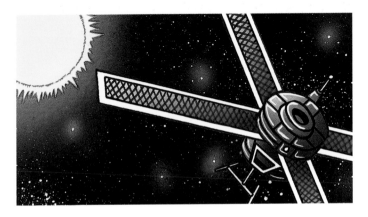

"Suddenly, at 3:03 P.M., it happened."

Blackout!
Sudden, dark
Working, thinking, fixing
Wires, switches, lines, circuits
Humming, glowing, shining
Sudden, bright
Light.